Forward and Credit

Pastor Benjamin Tomah

Much credit must go to my good and long-time friend Pastor Benjamin Tomah of Liberia Africa. Pastor Benjamin discovered value in what we had written long before we did. I often call him "The co-founder of ISOB." In 1998 Pastor Benjamin saw some of our writings before they were even books. I was intending to help him make disciples by sending him books by some famous authors. While he appreciated those books, he said he preferred what we had written. That shocked me! Pastor Benjamin has discipled many people and planted several churches, which expanded the Kingdom of God. Many have been saved as a result.

This in no way is meant to neglect hundreds, perhaps thousands, of other anointed ministers of God who have and are tirelessly publishing the Word through our books all over the world. While I do not have room here to write all their names, they know who they are and God knows how much their work has meant to the Kingdom of God.

1

Chapter 1
An Appetizer for Making Disciples

When the Lord saved me, I had already attempted to succeed in the world's system with everything that I had. I was 39 years old, it was 1979, and although on the surface things looked okay, inside I knew that I was not making life work. The Lord made some changes in my life, both in my relationships and in business, in order to put me on His path for my life.

Even then, I knew that I did not have the resources to make life work. I cried out desperately to Him for help with finances, family relationships, and ministry. I knew He had a calling on my life, but had no idea what that meant. I knew that God wanted me to have the "abundant life," and all I could do was to believe and invite Him to take over 100%. I loved the Word of God and spent hours every day consuming it. It began to change my life in many ways.

I will never forget watching a minister on television teach on Mark chapter 4, and how the Word of God planted in a human heart would bear fruit for everything we need, for life and godliness, 2 Peter 1:3. I grabbed that idea and lived by it. Little by little I could see God producing His fruit in my life, and that it would produce things and situations that I would not have had the power to do on my own. I knew this was Truth.

I also saw how this fruit did not grow quickly. Satan would war against the production of fruit in powerful ways. There was much suffering, but my wife Carol and I would not give in or give up because we knew that God meant what He said. Actually the suffering for the Words sake was part of entering into the Kingdom of God.

Acts 14:22 says,

> *"strengthening the souls of the disciples, exhorting* them *to continue in the faith, and*

From Thorns to Fruit
An Appetizer for Making Disciples

By Larry Chkoreff

First Printing Spring 2009
Revised October 2015
Version 1.9

Copyright © 2009 by Larry Chkoreff
Published by International School of the Bible (ISOB),
Marietta, Georgia, U.S.A.

For information on reproducing this book contact ISOB at:
Email address – info@isob-bible.org
The ISOB web site is www.isob-bible.org.

i

Table of Contents

saying, *"We must through many tribulations enter the kingdom of God.""*

Eventually things got better, little by little, and God showed up in marvelous ways. Now as I write this, over 32 years later, I can testify not only by the Word of God, but also by my own experience, that living life by bearing fruit is indeed the mystery of the Kingdom of God.

Best of all, during these past years, by focusing on hearing God speak and keeping my relationship fresh and vital with Him, my personal intimacy with Jesus has become very deep and satisfying. Even if I had nothing else in this world, just knowing Him at this deep and intimate level is more than enough!

No blurred distinctions.
Too many Christians get blurry eyed when they consider the Kingdom of God. Many believe that it is reserved for after we die. Some think it is for the "Millennium" as described in the Book of Revelation. However some do believe that it is for the now, and for the future.

However even among those, many blur the Kingdom of God with the kingdoms of this world. They feel that just improving our national governments will bring God's will and kingdom into this earth.

Satan offered the kingdoms of this earth to Jesus when he tempted Jesus as told in Luke chapter 4. Jesus passively admitted that all the kingdoms of this world belonged to Satan at that time. Revelation chapter 18 makes it clear, that taken together and named Mystery Babylon, all the kingdoms of this world will destroy themselves. Revelation chapter 11 also makes it clear that Jesus finally will rule in every area that the kingdoms of this world are now ruling. In my opinion that will not be by improving them from their present state but by allowing them to destroy themselves as stated in Revelation 18:1-13, which says,

"1 After these things I saw another angel coming down from heaven, having great authority, and the earth was illuminated with his glory.

2 And he cried mightily with a loud voice, saying, "Babylon the great is fallen, is fallen, and has become a dwelling place of demons, a prison for every foul spirit, and a cage for every unclean and hated bird!

3 "For all the nations have drunk of the wine of the wrath of her fornication, the kings of the earth have committed fornication with her, and the merchants of the earth have become rich through the abundance of her luxury."

4 And I heard another voice from heaven saying, "Come out of her, my people, lest you share in her sins, and lest you receive of her plagues.

5 "For her sins have reached to heaven, and God has remembered her iniquities.

6 "Render to her just as she rendered to you, and repay her double according to her works; in the cup which she has mixed, mix double for her.

7 "In the measure that she glorified herself and lived luxuriously, in the same measure give her torment and sorrow; for she says in her heart, 'I sit as queen, and am no widow, and will not see sorrow.'

8 "Therefore her plagues will come in one day--death and mourning and famine. And she will be utterly burned with fire, for strong is the Lord God who judges her.

9 "The kings of the earth who committed fornication and lived luxuriously with her will weep and lament for her, when they see the smoke of her burning,
10 "standing at a distance for fear of her torment, saying, 'Alas, alas, that great city Babylon, that mighty city! For in one hour your judgment has come.'
11 "And the merchants of the earth will weep and mourn over her, for no one buys their merchandise anymore:
12 "merchandise of gold and silver, precious stones and pearls, fine linen and purple, silk and scarlet, every kind of citron wood, every kind of object of ivory, every kind of object of most precious wood, bronze, iron, and marble;
13 "and cinnamon and incense, fragrant oil and frankincense, wine and oil, fine flour and wheat, cattle and sheep, horses and chariots, and bodies and souls of men."

Therefore we should not stand around and wait for our governments, our schools, our health care, or our finances to improve because our governments will improve. We need to repent, and turn to the Kingdom of God.

It is normally accepted that dictator and communist governments are often corrupt and offer no hope for their people. Why is this true? Simply because the dictators and the leaders are corrupt. It is the same even in a democratic government. While I love the United States of America, and I would rather live here than anywhere else in the world, our government is still of the world's system. I recognize that America is a very special government even in the history of the world; nevertheless it is only as good as the people in control. Who is in control in a democracy? The voters.

And you can be sure that the majority of the voters who rule most democracies in world history, including America, are corrupt.

Jesus told us to repent, which is to take a 180-degree turn, because the Kingdom of God is now at hand. He said to seek first His Kingdom and His righteousness, and all the things that non-believers sweat and work hard for will simply be added to us as fruit, Matthew 6:33. Not only will see fruit in our lives for our character, our provisions our ministry, but also our relationship with Jesus will be very real and tangible.

Chapter 2
The Mystery of The Kingdom of God

The mystery of the Kingdom of God.
Mark 4:11 says,
"And He said to them, "To you it has been given to know the mystery of the kingdom of God; but to those who are outside, all things come in parables.."

Jesus was telling His disciples and us that the simple Parable of the Sower contains the mystery of the Kingdom of God. This is not for theologians or religious people, this is for simple people, humble people, honest people, even uneducated people. It is spiritual agriculture. However we must be desperate and honest enough to hear God.

Jesus came to return us to normal.
Adam went from fruit to thorns and sweat. He ended up like the fig tree in Mark chapter 11 that Jesus dried up. Jesus was looking for fruit which was supposed to be on the tree along with the leaves. We can choose like Adam did between fruit or thorns and sweat. If you choose sweat you will end up like Adam did, looking great and prideful in your fig leaf, but having no fruit whatsoever.
Adam had the mandate to tend the garden, to be fruitful. God had provided the capital of a garden, not only in the natural, but also in Adam's heart. God promised that if Adam would come to the Tree of Life, the Word of God, daily, that God would speak in an intimate relationship, the spiritual seeds would be planted in his heart, and his life would be abundant though fruit bearing, both natural and spiritual.
However, between Adam and Eve, they decided that their own intelligence, intellect and strength was capable of making their life work for them without depending 100% on

7

the Word of God. That decision of theirs is what the Bible calls eating of the Tree of Knowledge of Good and Evil. That was and is the essence of sin.

The curse of thorns.

God had given Adam the blessing of perfect business capital, a garden that would bring forth perfect fruit. However, as we know, Adam wished to be independent. God had no other choice but to advise Adam that he, Adam, had chosen a curse and would have to now provide for himself among thorns and with sweat.

Genesis 2:15 says,

> *"15 Then the LORD God took the man and put him in the garden of Eden to tend and keep it."*

Genesis 3:17-19 says,

> *"17 Then to Adam He said, "Because you have heeded the voice of your wife, and have eaten from the tree of which I commanded you, saying, 'You shall not eat of it': "Cursed is the ground for your sake; In toil you shall eat of it All the days of your life.*
>
> *18 Both thorns and thistles it shall bring forth for you, And you shall eat the herb of the field.*
>
> *19 In the sweat of your face you shall eat bread Till you return to the ground, For out of it you were taken; For dust you are, And to dust you shall return.""*

Jesus bore our curse.

Mark 15:17 says,

> *"17 And they clothed Him with purple; and they twisted a crown of thorns, put it on His head.."*

We now have the great godly privilege to go back to "normal," and bear fruit without the curse and the thorns!

The New Testament Sabbath.
We are to rest from the works of our flesh, our sweat, and rest in the Word of God. Resting from the works of our flesh, that is the Sabbath that pleases God. We can rest because we know that the Word of God is a living seed and will produce.

Hebrews 4:1-12 says,

"1 Therefore, since a promise remains of entering His rest, let us fear lest any of you seem to have come short of it.

2 For indeed the gospel was preached to us as well as to them; but the word which they heard did not profit them, not being mixed with faith in those who heard it.

3 For we who have believed do enter that rest, as He has said: "So I swore in My wrath, 'They shall not enter My rest,'" although the works were finished from the foundation of the world.

4 For He has spoken in a certain place of the seventh day in this way: "And God rested on the seventh day from all His works";

5 and again in this place: "They shall not enter My rest."

6 Since therefore it remains that some must enter it, and those to whom it was first preached did not enter because of disobedience,

7 again He designates a certain day, saying in David, "Today," after such a long time, as it has been said: "Today, if you will hear His voice, Do not harden your hearts."

8 For if Joshua had given them rest, then He would not afterward have spoken of another day.

9 There remains therefore a rest for the people of God.

10 For he who has entered His rest has himself also ceased from his works as God did from His.

11 Let us therefore be diligent to enter that rest, lest anyone fall according to the same example of disobedience.

12 For the word of God is living and powerful, and sharper than any two-edged sword, piercing even to the division of soul and spirit, and of joints and marrow, and is a discerner of the thoughts and intents of the heart."

Isaiah 58:13, 14 says,

"13 "If you turn away your foot from the Sabbath, From doing your pleasure on My holy day, And call the Sabbath a delight, The holy day of the LORD honorable, And shall honor Him, not doing your own ways, Nor finding your own pleasure, Nor speaking your own words,

14 Then you shall delight yourself in the LORD; And I will cause you to ride on the high hills of the earth, And feed you with the heritage of Jacob your father. The mouth of the LORD has spoken.""

We must stay connected.

Entering the New Testament Sabbath involves continually doing what is needed to stay in God's presence [1],

---

[1] This is covered in detail in our book Grow or Die. http://www.isob-bible.org/openlessons.htm

to hear His Word, and to be guided by the Holy Spirit. Then God pulls us along in "His chariot" through the "abundant life" so that we experience what God has written, and completed, for our lives before the foundation of the earth.

The Rich Young Ruler and the One-Hour Man.

When Jesus encountered the Rich Young Ruler as recorded in Matthew chapter 19, the Ruler told Jesus that he had lived a near perfect life. His parents must have been very proud of him. He went to Temple and/or Synagogue on a regular basis, he kept all the commands he could, he did not have premarital sex, he did not steal, he told the truth, yet he knew that he was lacking something. Jesus asked him to give up his possessions and swap them for treasures. Possessions could be seen and held, they are the visible. However treasures are the invisible, they cannot be seen with the human eye. Had this man obeyed Jesus, he would have become very wealthy. However he could have had the wealth in such a way that it did not possess him. Jesus wanted him to become a fruit bearer by planting his money as seed, and indeed to give up control of his life. He asked him to destroy his idol.

The Ruler would not swap the visible for the invisible. He wanted to hang on to the kingdom of the world, and missed the Kingdom of God.

Look at the dialog.
Matthew 19:22-30
"22 But when the young man heard that saying, he went away sorrowful, for he had great possessions.

23 Then Jesus said to His disciples, "Assuredly, I say to you that it is hard for a rich man to enter the kingdom of heaven.

24 "And again I say to you, it is easier for a camel to go through the eye of a needle than for a rich man to enter the kingdom of God."

25 When His disciples heard it, they were greatly astonished, saying, "Who then can be saved?"

26 But Jesus looked at them and said to them, "With men this is impossible, but with God all things are possible."

27 Then Peter answered and said to Him, "See, we have left all and followed You. Therefore what shall we have?"

28 So Jesus said to them, "Assuredly I say to you, that in the regeneration, when the Son of Man sits on the throne of His glory, you who have followed Me will also sit on twelve thrones, judging the twelve tribes of Israel.

29 "And everyone who has left houses or brothers or sisters or father or mother or wife or children or lands, for My name's sake, shall receive a hundredfold, and inherit eternal life.

30 "But many who are first will be last, and the last first."

Notice that Jesus turned the conversation to focus on the main issue in verse 24, the Kingdom of God. Peter was astonished that this near perfect man was a reject for the Kingdom of God.

Then Jesus went on to explain what type of people would qualify for the Kingdom of God. He explained not only what *type* of people would qualify, but He also stated that some would enter the Kingdom of God before others depending upon their qualifications.

To explain this He told a parable of a landowner who went to the market place in order to hire workers for his vineyard. He found, in my opinion, the strongest most qualified of the pick, and hired him for a standard day's wages, called a denarius. Then as the day went on, and after seeing, on four more occasions, that the harvest required more labor, he went back to the marketplace to hire more workers to work just a portion of a day. He did not promise how much he would pay these last four workers, but guaranteed that he would be fair. The last person he hired only worked for one hour. We call him the One Hour Man. He most likely was the least qualified of all the workers. Maybe he was even handicapped so that no one wanted to hire him.

Matthew 20:8-16 says,

"8 "So when evening had come, the owner of the vineyard said to his steward, 'Call the laborers and give them their wages, beginning with the last to the first.'

9 "And when those came who were hired about the eleventh hour, they each received a denarius.

10 "But when the first came, they supposed that they would receive more; and they likewise received each a denarius.

11 "And when they had received it, they complained against the landowner,

12 "saying, 'These last men have worked only one hour, and you made them equal to us who have borne the burden and the heat of the day.'

13 "But he answered one of them and said, 'Friend, I am doing you no wrong. Did you not agree with me for a denarius?

14 'Take what is yours and go your way. I wish to give to this last man the same as to you.

15 'Is it not lawful for me to do what I wish
with my own things? Or is your eye evil because
I am good?'
16 "So the last will be first, and the first last.
For many are called, but few chosen.""

Notice, the One Hour Man got "paid" first. Pay, in this
parable, is the inheritance of the Kingdom of God. The least
qualified, the most broken, the most desperate and
dependent obtains the privilege of bearing fruit in the
Kingdom of God before others. God has a way of choosing
what the world considers the least qualified.

1 Corinthians 1:18-21
"18 For the message of the cross is
foolishness to those who are perishing, but to us
who are being saved it is the power of God.
19 For it is written: "I will destroy the
wisdom of the wise, And bring to nothing the
understanding of the prudent."
20 Where is the wise? Where is the scribe?
Where is the disputer of this age? Has not God
made foolish the wisdom of this world?
21 For since, in the wisdom of God, the world
through wisdom did not know God, it pleased
God through the foolishness of the message
preached to save those who believe."

1 Corinthians 1:25-29
"25 Because the foolishness of God is wiser
than men, and the weakness of God is stronger
than men.
26 For you see your calling, brethren, that
not many wise according to the flesh, not many
mighty, not many noble, are called.

27 But God has chosen the foolish things of the world to put to shame the wise, and God has chosen the weak things of the world to put to shame the things which are mighty;

28 and the base things of the world and the things which are despised God has chosen, and the things which are not, to bring to nothing the things that are,

29 that no flesh should glory in His presence."

Wait for the fruit of Isaac instead of producing an Ishmael.

A quote from Watchman Nee from A Table in the Wilderness- June 23. [2]

I will give thee thanks forever, because thou hast done it: and I will wait on thy name, for it is good. Psalm 52:9.

The test of time is the hardest test of all. Yet only by learning to wait for God do we find ourselves involved in something really done by him. Ten years after he had believed God for a son, Abram felt he could wait no longer. He knew God intended him to have an heir so he sought to provide one, and Ishmael was the result. It was not Abram's motive that was wrong, but his starting point. He felt he could still do something to produce a child, as indeed he could, and did. At eighty-six he yet had that capacity.

There followed a further long wait, until at the age of a hundred Abraham could no longer do even this; his body was "as good as dead"

---

[2] Nee, Watchman. A Table In The Wilderness. Tyndale House Publishers. Wheaton, IL. 1965.

(Romans 4:19). It was to such a man, powerless now in himself to please God, that the marvelous gift of grace came in the person of Isaac. This was wholly God's doing and well worth waiting for. To have God do his own work through us, even once, is better than a lifetime of human striving.

Chapter 3
Hearing God Speak

We cannot bear fruit without hearing God speak and obeying what He says.
There can be no seed planted without directly and personally hearing God speak. When Jesus said that we need ears to hear, He was not speaking about the natural ears on our head. He was referring to our spiritual ears.

Why is it that some cannot hear?
Isaiah chapter 6 combined with Mark chapter 4 will give us the answer to that question.

When Isaiah "saw the Lord" as recorded in Isaiah chapter 6, several things resulted.

1. Isaiah knew himself to be a man undone and unclean.
Isaiah 6:5 says,
"5 So I said: "Woe is me, for I am undone! Because I am a man of unclean lips, And I dwell in the midst of a people of unclean lips; For my eyes have seen the King, The LORD of hosts.""

2. God cleansed him.
Isaiah 6:7 says,
"7 And he touched my mouth with it, and said: "Behold, this has touched your lips; Your iniquity is taken away, And your sin purged.""

3. God sent him to preach a very unusual message.
Isaiah 6:8-11 says,
"8 Also I heard the voice of the Lord, saying: "Whom shall I send, And who will go for Us?" Then I said, "Here am I! Send me."

9 And He said, "Go, and tell this people: 'Keep on hearing, but do not understand; Keep on seeing, but do not perceive.'

10 "Make the heart of this people dull, And their ears heavy, And shut their eyes; Lest they see with their eyes, And hear with their ears, And understand with their heart, And return and be healed."

11 Then I said, "Lord, how long?" And He answered: "Until the cities are laid waste and without inhabitant, The houses are without a man, The land is utterly desolate,"

I believe what God had told Isaiah in answer to Isaiah's question, "How long do I have to preach this strange message?" was, "Until My people are desperate enough to be able to hear My Word."

Now compare this to when Jesus quoted Isaiah in Mark chapter 4 as He was discussing the mystery of the Kingdom of God being embedded in the Parable of the Sower, i.e., hearing God with the result of a seed planted in one's heart.

Mark 4:10-12 (Amplified Bible) says,

10 And as soon as He was alone, those who were around Him, with the Twelve [apostles], began to ask Him about the parables.

11 And He said to them, To you has been entrusted the mystery of the kingdom of God [that is, the secret counsels of God which are hidden from the ungodly]; but for those outside [of our circle] everything becomes a parable,

12 In order that they may [indeed] look and look but not see and perceive, and may hear and hear but not grasp and comprehend, lest haply they should turn again, and it [their willful rejection of the truth] should be forgiven them.

Notice, Jesus said that "willful rejection of truth" would cause people to not hear.

God said to Isaiah that people could not hear until they are desperate enough. There you go! Be gut level honest with yourself first, then with God. Submit yourself to God continually until, with His help, you become totally desperate to depend upon the Word. Then, my brothers and sisters, you will have intimate contact with God, He will plant His Word into your heart, and if you obey and stand, you will see God's fruit in and through your life, AMEN!

Chapter 4
Jesus' Command to Make Disciples

Jesus said to go make disciples.
We have the privilege of confronting people with such good news!
Most people are hurting in one way or another. People have felt needs. It may be sickness, finance, family, addictions, inner wounds, or a host of other issues. We can tell them that we know that the kingdoms of this world cannot provide the answers they need, but that Jesus said that if we would seek first the Kingdom of God, that He, the King, would take care of our needs. People will listen because most have overwhelming needs, and you have the seeds for the needs!
Making disciples is our mission.
Matthew 28:19 says,
> *""Go therefore and make disciples of all the nations, baptizing them in the name of the Father and of the Son and of the Holy Spirit."*

What is a disciple as Jesus meant it?
It means to be under the discipline of a master, Jesus; to live your life like He does. He lives by faith, He lives by fruit, He is holy, and He continually looks at the unseen and gives more value to it than He does the seen. His mind is disciplined to live by the Word of God and to depend totally on the Word, even beyond what He sees with His eyes. Jesus lived His life on earth by constantly needing to hear the Father speak.

> John 5:30 says,
> *"30 "I can of Myself do nothing. As I hear, I judge; and My judgment is righteous, because I do not seek My own will but the will of the Father who sent Me."*

In order to live in this manner, one must discipline his or her mind. It all starts there with choice, the will or volition. We must continue to focus on the invisible truths and facts of the Bible by memorizing, quoting and meditating upon Scripture and fellowshipping with the Holy Spirit and Jesus. Our minds can fight against us by "begging" us to focus on our problems, but we can take charge as in 2 Corinthians 10:4, which says,

"4 For the weapons of our warfare are not carnal but mighty in God for pulling down strongholds,"

Also, 2 Corinthians 4:18 says,

"18 while we do not look at the things which are seen, but at the things which are not seen. For the things which are seen are temporary, but the things which are not seen are eternal."

Being a disciple means being a fruit bearer.
John 15:8 says when we are fruit bearers Jesus is made real through us to others. We don't have to try to show Jesus to people if we are fruit bearers, God will do it through us. The word glorified in this Scripture means to be revealed.
John 15:8 says,

"8 "By this My Father is glorified, that you bear much fruit; so you will be My disciples."

Being a fruit bearer brings joy and pleases Jesus.
John 15:11 says,

"11 "These things I have spoken to you, that My joy may remain in you, and that your joy may be full."

What kind of fruit?

Some people think that fruit for the Kingdom of God is limited to ministry, souls saved and disciples made. Clearly Scripture includes ministry as fruit, but so many people limit it to that.

Scripture testifies that God wants our entire lives to be the result of fruit bearing. That is living in the Kingdom of God.

The Ark of the Covenant gives us a peek.

Since our bodies are now the Temple of God, therefore God's Ark must also be in us, 1 Corinthians 6:19.

The Ark contains the following potential for fruit:

1. The Law. Our character. That law of God is now in our hearts. Fruit of the Spirit is the first and most important fruit.

2. Manna. Our provisions. God wants to provide for all of our earthly needs supernaturally by planting His seeds in our hearts. I can personally testify to the truth and experience of this.

3. Aaron's Rod. Our ministry. Aaron's almond rod is the only one of the twelve rods left in the Temple overnight that budded. It is important to remember that none of these almond rods had any roots, therefore the buds were supernatural.

One of the fruits of a disciple is to plant new bodies of believers, or churches.

I believe that this is Scriptural, but it is also our experience since 1997. As disciples learn about bearing fruit, many of them simply plant a new church, or a body of believers. That may included a Bible study, or home group, or other type of gathering. The fruit from that new gathering is not only more disciples, but also the salvation of people who have not known Christ before.

Chapter 5
God Is A Fruit Bearer

God is a fruit bearer.
The prophecies of the Old Testament are not simply a foretelling of what God knew was going to happen. The speaking of the prophecies were the seeds that *caused* everything to happen. What is going on today is actually the fruit born by people hearing what God spoke as seeds. The testimony of Jesus is the spirit of prophecy.

Revelation 19:10 says,

> *"And I fell at his feet to worship him. But he said to me, "See that you do not do that! I am your fellow servant, and of your brethren who have the testimony of Jesus. Worship God! For the testimony of Jesus is the spirit of prophecy.""*

To make a disciple means to cause someone to live his or her life as a fruit bearer.
It is to cause someone to return to normal and live like Adam did before he forsook the Word and started living by his sweat.

How do we do that?
There are many ways, and I in no way wish to limit God or to promote what we are doing at the International School of The Bible (ISOB) as something special or the only way. However, knowing that what we have been doing since 1998 is field-tested and is bearing much fruit, I will share with you how that works. If this interests you, then you may contact us to see how we may join together on this path.

First, you can simply tell someone the message in this booklet, about how God wants them to have their needs provided for by fruit, by seeking first His Kingdom. Tell them to allow God to plant the Word seeds in their hearts, and to hang on for as long as it takes to see those seeds bear fruit.

Also, you can be a "publisher" of the Word of God. Writers write, printers print, but publishers distribute. God planted one of the seeds in my heart for this ministry by speaking to me Psalms 68:11, which says,

> *"11 The Lord gave the word: great was the company of those that published it."*

Notice is says that the army, or company of those who published the Word was great! The word *great* means a great and mighty and abundant multitude. At the present time in 2009 at this writing, there is a multitude of tens of thousands of people publishing, or distributing the Word through our books. A pastor may receive 100 books. Then the disciples he makes receives several of those books and in turn goes and makes more disciples. We have lost track of how many are in this "company" at the present time. It amazes my imagination of what God is doing by bearing fruit in our lives at ISOB! We never even prayed for anything this big, widespread and powerful. It is all Him, and He receives all the glory, because I know how limited and helpless I am in myself, in my natural flesh abilities. We all have received an anointing from the Lord to be a "publisher" of the Word according to Psalm 68:11.

As of this writing in 2011 there are 500,000 of our books in print and in the hands of disciples in over 45 nations.

To be a publisher of the Word, people do not have to see our face.

Many ministers believe that the only way they can affect people is to show up in person. Don't get me wrong, I know that God has an anointing for many people to have them show up personally to evangelize and to disciple. But that is not for all of us. You will be making disciples through others that you may never meet.

The apostle Paul, as recorded in Acts chapter 20 set an interesting example for us. He was sailing to a city named Miletus. The elders from Ephesus asked him to stop to see them. Instead, he sent for them to meet him in Miletus, for he was in a hurry on his way to Jerusalem. While he was speaking to them, on his way to Jerusalem to suffer even more. Further in his conversation with them, he told them "you will see my face no more." Then he told them that instead of coming back to minister to them that he would commend them to the word of God. That means that he would entrust their wellbeing and spiritual growth not to his own personal preaching, but to the Word that he would leave with them. Notice the wellbeing would even prevail when evil men and awful tribulations would attack them. I think I would rather have had the Book of Ephesians than Paul showing up once a month to preach to me! How about you?

Moses' father-in-law had the right idea.
As recorded in Exodus chapter 18, Moses was overwhelmed with his ministry, and the people's needs were not being met. Moses was frustrated as were the people.

Moses' father-in-law Jethro advised him to stop attempting to minister to all the people personally, but rather to spend his time with leaders, train them, so that they may extend his ministry to the multitudes. Perhaps Moses' "burnout" here sowed some bad seeds with the people that would bear destructive fruit at a later time. It would be natural for people whose needs are not being met to begin to provide for themselves. The people were connected to God through Moses, and by seeing his frustration, possibly they felt suddenly disconnected from God, alone, unfulfilled and vulnerable, Later, in Moses' absence, they made their own god.

In essence Moses was living by the sweat of his brow which caused burnout in his ministry and discouragement in his people. However, by following his father-in-law's advice, he reproduced himself into the leaders who were then empowered to minister to the people. Moses became a fruit bearer and a publisher of the Word. Also he enabled many other to do the same. We need to follow God's plan to do the same.

Exodus 18:14-24 (Amplified) says,

14 When Moses' father-in-law saw all that he was doing for the people, he said, What is this that you do for the people? Why do you sit alone, and all the people stand around you from morning till evening?

15 Moses said to his father-in-law, Because the people come to me to inquire of God.

16 When they have a dispute they come to me, and I judge between a man and his neighbor, and I make them know the statutes of God and His laws.

17 Moses' father-in-law said to him, The thing that you are doing is not good.

18 You will surely wear out both yourself and this people with you, for the thing is too heavy for you; you are not able to perform it all by yourself.

19 Listen now to [me]; I will counsel you, and God will be with you. You shall represent the people before God, bringing their cases and causes to Him,

20 Teaching them the decrees and laws, showing them the way they must walk and the work they must do.

21 Moreover, you shall choose able men from all the people--God-fearing men of truth who hate unjust gain--and place them over thousands, hundreds, fifties, and tens, to be their rulers.

22 And let them judge the people at all times; every great matter they shall bring to you, but every small matter they shall judge. So it will be easier for you, and they will bear the burden with you.

23 If you will do this, and God so commands you, you will be able to endure [the strain], and all these people also will go to their [tents] in peace.

24 So Moses listened to and heeded the voice of his father-in-law and did all that he had said.

25 Moses chose able men out of all Israel and made them heads over the people, rulers of thousands, of hundreds, of fifties, and of tens.

26 And they judged the people at all times; the hard cases they brought to Moses, but every small matter they decided themselves.

27 Then Moses let his father-in-law depart, and he went his way into his own land.

This I learned from the shadow of a tree.
That to and fro did sway upon a wall;
My shadow self, my influence may fall
Where I can never be.

Dwight M. Kitch

Chapter 6
God's Math

If you are a fruit bearer you will experience God's math!
I discovered something about God during the past several years that I have known in my heart and mind, but have not experienced before. As fruit is developed, it carries more and more seeds that are planted into the ground. Try to imagine this. It would be difficult to do the math of how much fruit one tree could bear in a ten-year period. It would be difficult to count all the fruit, then count their seeds that they bear, and keep adding and adding.

I have discovered that adding does not work, neither does multiplication when calculating God's method of increase. I am not even sure that exponential increase is adequate, but it is the biggest thing I can get my brain around.

I learned this by the Lord teaching me about the House of David. I do not have room here to go into the entire story and history of the House of David, but I will attempt to abbreviate it and still keep its proper context.

God told David that He would build him a house that would be used to bless the poor. David did bless the poor, but his descendants did not. Therefore God spoke and took the anointing away from them. However He did speak through the Prophets in Jeremiah and other books, that the House of David would one day be resorted. However this time it would be in the "Last days" and the Gentiles could also partake of that blessing and anointing.

Amos 9:11-15 says,

"11 "On that day I will raise up The tabernacle of David, which has fallen down, And repair its damages; I will raise up its ruins, And rebuild it as in the days of old;

12 That they may possess the remnant of Edom, And all the Gentiles who are called by My name," Says the LORD who does this thing.

13 "Behold, the days are coming," says the LORD, "When the plowman shall overtake the reaper, And the treader of grapes him who sows seed; The mountains shall drip with sweet wine, And all the hills shall flow with it.

14 I will bring back the captives of My people Israel; They shall build the waste cities and inhabit them; *They shall plant vineyards and drink wine from them; They shall also make gardens and eat fruit from them.*

15 I will plant them in their land, And no longer shall they be pulled up From the land I have given them," Says the LORD your God."

In Acts 15:13-17, when the Apostles realized that Peter had brought Gentiles to Jesus, James stated that this is what Amos spoke of in Amos chapter 9.

But it does not end there back in the First Century. Jesus said to the Church of Philadelphia in Revelation that He has the Key of David, inferring that this anointing is for us today.

Revelation 3:7 says,

"7 "And to the angel of the church in Philadelphia write, 'These things says He who is holy, He who is true, "He who has the key of David, He who opens and no one shuts, and shuts and no one opens":"

The House of David, taking care of the poor, was lost for centuries. However Jesus spoke to us through the Church of Philadelphia in Revelation 3:7, that He has the key of David for us.

Amos chapter 9 says that the increase of the House of David in the last days will be as the plowman overtaking the reapers, etc. In other words, not addition, not multiplication, but exponential, and beyond, increase. This feeding is not only for natural food for those who are poor, but also for those who are poor in spirit who need spiritual food.

Chapter 7
Testimonies

Disciple making in Africa.
Brother Larry:
For many years and many ways unknowingly people have followed practices that worked against the goal that God wanted them to pursue, the goal of making disciples. But gradually, the Holy Spirit graciously has and is opening the eyes through ISOB to see making disciples as the key to in building and preparing the church for the kingdom.

We should question every thing we have been taught and believed in light with the word of God, some people are so proud of their traditions, and their are tens of thousands of denominations in the world today, and as result of peoples pride, God resists them because He resists the proud.

Pastors, overseers and elders goals of making disciples should shape every thing in our ministry. Pastors and other leaders let us set an example of obedience as true disciples of Jesus Christ. Our example speaks ten times louder than our sermons.

Most of the great Christian leaders of the past are not remembered for their sermons, but for their sacrifice, their example inspires many people long after they are gone.

Let us be strong by His grace.
A Pastor in Africa

Dear brother Larry,
Thank you for all what you're doing in the Lords service. The system I am using in the discipleship program, is to fast first. Then I hold

31

seminars with church leaders to train them on how to use our books and to understand the message in the books. Then we give books to pastors and other church leaders.

We organize small groups in churches, with families in the home, at schools and in Bible study meetings. We also visit people in their working place, hospitals and prisons etc., but all this can only be done through the one who gives us strength.

Let us keep ourselves in the Lords service and may the Lord give us strength, courage and wisdom to serve Him.

A Pastor in Africa

Disciple making by Maurice Odhiambo, Nairobi Kenya.
What can YOU do with a Grow Or Die Book?

Not much until you study it and allow the Holy Spirit to use it to minister to you personally and help you to approach the teachings as something that you desperately need for your own application before you give it out. When you do so with prayer, the Holy Spirit empowers that little book. When the Holy Spirit runs with your act of faith big things happen . . . remember the boy who gave Jesus 2 small fish and 5 loaves of bread? Jesus accepted the boy's small gift and used it to feed thousands. Then the Lord will feel us and we can experience the overflow that will eventually reach, touch and transform others, this is when we find ourselves traveling day and night and sharing and training disciples for Jesus using Grow Or Die book in many locations, cities, nations and the world.

During these Grow Or Die one on one sharing seminars, conferences, etc., we have seen GOD use Grow Or Die and other ISOB Materials to:

Encourage *an unbeliever to fall into the arms of a loving God.*

Invite *seekers to our church family.*

Persuade *the reader/student to repent and put his or her faith in Christ.*

Nudge *the bored Christians into active service of the Lord.*

Strengthen *people's faith as they partner with Christ in the greatest endeavor of the world.*

Produce *true and effective disciples and leaders for Jesus*

ISOB is the new wave that God is using to prepare the blameless and perfect Bride for His Son Jesus Christ. We in Kenya are proud to be part of this new powerful move of God through ISOB worldwide. We are tools in His hands through ISOB.

Maurice and Benter Odhiambo

ISOB - Kenya

Behind enemy lines.
There have been many testimonies that I dare not quote here on how our books somehow "invaded" dark strongholds in least reached areas and brought people to the saving knowledge of Jesus. Many of these strongholds were of religions that are at enmity with Christianity.

One entire kingdom (within the borders of a nation) in East Africa was invaded by our books when the king called to an ISOB representative to find out "what in the world is the big deal about the books he had heard about." The king bowed his knee to Jesus and ordered his religious ministers to utilize the ISOB books.

Prisoners on death row in a Kenya prison were put back into society by the judge who had condemned them after seeing a radical change in their lives.

Unreached areas in the South American Andes, including the ancient Incas have been reached through ISOB books.

Why the books?

I am not a typical writer. Our books are not based upon theology, although theology is indeed embedded within them. I never wrote a book for the purpose of selling it, although the Lord has led me in recent years to make them available for purchase.

Our books evolved from God taking my wife and I through very difficult overcoming times in our lives. It is just a natural thing for me to write down what I have learned and how God dealt with me. Therefore our books are testimonies backed by the Word of God as the Lord has taken us through difficult circumstances.

Watchman Nee has said,

> "Who is a minister of the Word? One who translates Christ into the Bible. He tells people of the Christ he has gotten to know, using the words of the Bible. The Holy Spirit then translates these words back into Christ in those who receive them."

The GPS strategy.
Glorify God
Prepare Disciples
Send Missionaries

GPS is a method of reaching hard to reach or unreached areas with the Gospel and discipleship. A local pastor developed this program.

He targets churches that desire to have a missions outreach. Then he trains the pastor and a few leaders who them proceed to make disciples. From the discipleship process certain people rise that are called to be missionaries to nearby or far away areas. He utilizes the ISOB Grow or Die book and other materials for this training.

We consider this the "rifle approach" as opposed to the "shotgun approach." Wide distribution of many books can be very expensive, and is sometimes very effective. However the GPS method utilizes fewer recourses in books and is very effective in reaching unreached and least reached areas.

The power of the printed Word of God. February 3 - Streams in The Desert. [3]

So shall my word be that goeth forth out of my mouth: it shall not return unto me void, but it shall accomplish that which I please, and it shall prosper in the thing whereto I sent it (Isa. 55:11).

The life is not in the sower, but in the seed. Even if an infidel scattered the Scriptures, he would only be exploding his own battlements.

For in scattering divine literature we liberate thistledown, laden with precious seed, which, blown by the winds of the Spirit, floats over the world. The printed page never flinches, never shows cowardice; it is never tempted to compromise; it never tires, never grows disheartened; it travels cheaply, and requires no hired hall; it works while we sleep; it never loses its temper; and it works long after we are dead. The printed page is a visitor which gets inside the home, and stays there; it always catches a man in the right mood, for it speaks to him only when he

---

[3]Mrs. Charles E. Cowman. Streams In The Desert. Daybreak Books. Grand Rapids, MI 1925.

is reading it; it always sticks to what it has said, and never answers back; and it is bait left permanently in the pool.

Luther wrote a pamphlet on Galatians, which, falling into Bunyan's hands, converted him; and several hundred translations of Pilgrim's Progress have been issued. More than 150,000,000 copies of Spurgeon's sermons have gone into circulation. Nor is even the political influence of the printed page measurable. A young Frenchman who had been wounded at the siege of Saint Quentin was languishing on a pallet in the hospital when a tract that lay on the coverlet caught his eye. He read it and was converted by it The monument of that man may be seen before the Church of the Consistory in Paris, standing with a Bible in his hand— Admiral Coligny, the leader of the Reformation in France. But the tract had not yet finished its work. It was read by Coligny's nurse, a Sister of Mercy, who penitently placed it in the hands of the Lady Abbess, and she, too, was converted by it She fled from France to the Palatinate, where she met a young Hollander and became his wife. The influence which she had upon that man reacted upon the whole continent of Europe, for he was William of Orange, who became the champion of liberty and Protestantism in the Netherlands.

The printed page is deathless: you can destroy one, but the press can reproduce millions; as often as it is martyred, it is raised: the ripple started by a given tract can widen down the centuries until it bears upon the great

*white throne. Its very mutilation can be its
sowing. P. Panton*

We can be as olive trees as in Zechariah chapter 4, who feed the body of Christ by the dripping of our oil. We can be as the woman in Mark chapter 14 who poured out her oil, her very substance, on Jesus' body. When we do something for His Body here on earth, it feels good to Him.

Other titles by Larry Chkoreff

Grow or Die
Free To Be You
Has Your King Died?
Junk to Jewels
Be Real With God
The Blood of The Everlasting Covenant
Living By Faith In A Broken World
Job's Journey
Thorns to Fruit
Who Is The Lamb?
Is There A New World Coming?
A Vision for Marriage
Hearing God's Voice
The Psalms One Business Owner
Speak The Word.
Power Team for Kids (download)
Leadership – The Secret

www.ingramcontent.com/pod-product-compliance
Lightning Source LLC
Chambersburg PA
CBHW060637030426
42337CB00018B/3391